DIOR

STYLE ICON

The Defining
Looks *from*
a Legendary
Fashion
House

STYLE
ICON

DIOR

DAN JONES

ILLUSTRATED
BY SANDRA SUY

Hardie Grant

BOOKS

INTRODUCTION
A Star is Born

In 1946, on Rue du Faubourg Saint-Honoré in Paris, a young Christian Dior found a tiny metal star. He was on his way to meet the cotton king of France, the millionaire Marcel Boussac, who had factories sitting empty after the war, and the future was unwritten. Dior, however, knew exactly what the star meant. A lifelong devotee of fortune-telling and omens, Dior felt it could only have signified one thing: he was on the right path. At first, Boussac wanted Dior to resurrect Philippe et Gaston, a once great but failed fashion house, but the young designer declined. Instead, inspired perhaps by his friend and colleague Pierre Balmain, he asked if he might create a new fashion house in his own name. The star omen was right: Boussac agreed, and the House of Dior was founded.

Dior drew on his rich experience with couturiers Robert Piguet and Lucien Lelong, his circle of achingly cool Parisian friends, his love of art and gastronomy, and his flower-filled, middle-class childhood to inform his ideas. He set about creating a dream team of traditional artisans and well-connected female fashion patrons, noting that a fortune-teller had once told him that 'women would make his success'. His debut collection was daring, the perfect remedy for post-war malaise, and deftly anticipated the zeitgeist.

In retrospect, the years 1947–57 are thought of as the pinnacle of French haute couture, with Christian Dior at the forefront of the art form. In 1952, he thought back to the tiny metal star on Rue du Faubourg Saint-Honoré and created a subtle print for his Bonne Étoile haute couture dress. Ever since, Dior's star has magicked its way in and out of countless collections, inspiring the great couturier's six successors in many ways.

As the House of Dior contemplates its eighth decade, *Dior: Style Icon* celebrates the ground-breaking couturier, his idyllic early childhood, Parisian highs and wartime lows, and the star-powered beginnings of an iconic fashion house that continues to shine brightly.

THE
NEW
LOOK

CHAPTER ONE

(1947–51)

THE ORIGINAL
Christian Dior

From his early childhood in Les Rhumbs, the Dior family's pale pink house with grey gravelling on the delightful Normandy coast, to his youth and teenage years in Paris, Christian Dior (1905–57) was always drawn to elegance and glamour. He could be 'amused for hours by anything that was sparkling, elaborate, flowery, or frivolous,' he wrote in his autobiography, *Dior by Dior* (1956); and he could see beauty in everything.

The second of Maurice and Madeleine Dior's five children, Christian was sent to study in Paris, but soon swapped political science for hanging out with the creative and intellectual in-crowd – and who wouldn't? 'We were just a simple gathering of painters, writers, musicians and designers,' wrote Dior, 'under the aegis of Jean Cocteau and Max Jacob.' In 1928, Dior's father helped him to finance a small gallery where he and a friend sold pieces by Pablo Picasso, but it closed three years later when catastrophe struck: Dior's mother and brother died, and the Great Depression sent his family into bankruptcy.

By then, Christian was in his mid-20s. He lost his apartment, had to lodge with friends, and his poor diet saw him contract tuberculosis and force him into a year-long period of convalescence. It is easy to underestimate how humbled he was; everything had gone wrong, and he needed a reset. He visited his father in the small Provençal farmhouse to which he had retired, spent time with his little sister, Christine, and drew hundreds of sketches, the first imaginings of fashion and accessory designs. But the reality of the family's situation meant his sketches weren't just whimsy; Christian realised he might have to help support his father and siblings. He famously sold his first sketch for 120 francs – a not insignificant amount – and buoyed up by this modest success, he returned to Paris to present to the haute couture houses.

By 1935, Dior had sold his drawings to milliners and couturiers, including Balenciaga, Jean Patou, Paquin and Schiaparelli, and worked as an illustrator for *Le Figaro* newspaper. Eventually, in 1937, Swiss couturier Robert Piguet commissioned Dior's designs, hiring him full-time a year later. Then came a decade with Lucien Lelong. Both he and Piguet were Dior's mentors of sorts, whom he would come to surpass.

DIOR'S MENTORS

Robert Piguet and Lucien Lelong

It was Dior's friend Georges Geoffroy who introduced him to the 'prince of fashion', the Swiss couturier Robert Piguet. Geoffroy was everyone who was anyone's interior designer, and Piguet's Parisian couture salons had been given the Geoffroy touch. Soon Piguet purchased some of Dior's designs and added them to one of his collections; Dior was thrilled. It was 1937, just before the Second World War, and although Dior had already had some success with his hat designs, he now felt as though he had finally made it: 'I was no longer a humble designer who hung about waiting-rooms, but a designer whose name was known.'

A year later, he was asked to join Piguet's in-house team. He was delighted at the offer, excited to learn the 'mysterious means' of how to turn 'an idea into a dress'. His profile began to rise, he made friends with Piguet's clients, and was introduced to Carmel Snow, the fashion editor at *Harper's Bazaar*, who was among the first people of influence to notice Dior's extraordinary talent. 'I really began to think that I had arrived,' he said.

But then, in 1939, world war broke out and Dior was 'rudely taken from my atmosphere of chiffon and *paillettes* [sequins]' and mobilised to central France to undertake farming duties. Although it was a world away from his life of fashion, to his surprise he loved working on the land, and a year later – when Paris came under German occupation – he moved in with his father and sister in southern France and continued to grow produce. But then came another opportunity. Even though the capital was occupied, the French couture houses were tentatively reopening, and Dior soon returned to Paris and connected with the man who would become his second mentor, Lucien Lelong. Working alongside another young upstart, Pierre Balmain, Dior found it like being at couture school, honing his craft and making more connections. When Paris was liberated at the end of the war, he, like everyone else, found he had changed. 'I wonder if my parents would have recognised me at the end of 1945,' he wrote, 'when the adventure of Christian Dior was just beginning. I scarcely recognised myself.'

A NEW LOOK

Christian Dior's legendary debut

On 12 February 1947, a bitterly cold day, a glamorous audience waited impatiently in a soft haze of cigarette smoke, exclusive *parfums* and nervous chatter in the salons of Christian Dior at 30 Avenue Montaigne. The Second World War had ended two years previously, the City of Light was still mired in post-war gloom, and the assembled audience of journalists, celebrities and private clients was hungry for something new. They had gathered at the design house, which had opened only months before, to view Dior's haute couture spring/summer collection, unaware they were about to play a part in fashion history.

Eventually, 'the first girl came out, stepping fast, switching with a provocative swinging movement, knocking over ashtrays,' wrote *Vogue*'s Bettina Ballard. Animated and theatrical, both the models and Dior's collection seemed wonderfully out of step with the grey mood of the time. He rejected both the pre-war style of the 1920s and 1930s – that slinky, shapeless flapper look – and the utilitarian dullness of wartime workwear, and offered something hyper-feminine, voluminous and confidently glamorous. The shape was the Carolle, or the Figure 8: wide in the shoulders and hips, but nipped in at the waist, and it set hearts racing. Dior hoped it might be 'the return to an ideal of civilised happiness', and within a few breathless moments, fashion had changed forever.

After the show, Carmel Snow, now editor-in-chief of *Harper's Bazaar* and a friend of Dior, said: '*It's quite a revolution, dear Christian! Your dresses have such a new look!*' And she wasn't the only fashion fan somewhat shaken by the couture designer's debut. 'The audience knew that Dior had created a New Look,' wrote Ballard in her report, perhaps paraphrasing Snow, '[and] we were witness to a revolution in fashion.'

THE BAR SUIT

An hourglass silhouette

Dior's first collection was the designer's antidote to post-war cultural apathy; what might he do, he wondered, to move his industry on from its pessimism and short-sightedness? War was over but 'traces of it were all around me', he wrote in *Dior by Dior*, 'damaged buildings, devastated countryside, rationing, the black market, and the less serious, but of more immediate interest to me, hideous fashions.' After being demobbed in 1942, Dior re-entered the fashion scene with unshakable optimism. 'An unhappy chapter of my life had ended. On the fresh, still unblemished page before me, I hoped to record nothing but happiness.' Little wonder, then, that his debut collection, five years later, seemed so surprising and uplifting.

Dior had a theme for each collection at the beginning of his couture career – it was the Carolle/Figure 8 silhouette in 1947 – but many other pieces caught the imagination of the audience. Among them was the Bar Suit jacket, almost architectural in design and generously rendered in ivory silk shantung. The button-up, basque-cut jacket had soft shoulders, a petite stand-up collar, and an impossibly tiny waist with generous peplum, padded at the hip to suggest a full, voluptuous figure: femininity and fun in overdrive. Paired with a black, pleated skirt, designed with its own dramatic proportions, the resulting Figure 8 silhouette was a perfect hourglass balanced on high heels. The Bar Suit (which took its name, apropos of nothing, from the bar at the Hôtel Plaza Athénée, one of Dior's favourite haunts) was an immediate hit, commissioned and copied endlessly, its shape echoing through more than 20 of Dior's own couture collections.

'DEEP IN EVERY
HEART SLUMBERS
A DREAM, AND
THE COUTURIER
KNOWS IT:
EVERY WOMAN
IS A PRINCESS.'

Christian Dior

THE ORIGINAL MISS DIOR

Heroine of the Resistance

Christian Dior's seminal first show in 1947 was also the debut of his first fragrance. The salon at 30 Avenue Montaigne was spritzed with a new perfume with a top note of galbanum – green and verdant-smelling, a floral heart of jasmine and Grasse rose absolute, and patchouli essence at its base. He called it Miss Dior, inspired by his sister, Catherine, the youngest of his four siblings and an award-winning Resistance heroine.

With his house in order and the excitement around his debut collection still mounting, Dior quickly expanded the brand. With his partner Jacques Rouet, he signed several licence agreements – rather novel at the time – and by 1948, deals for stockings, furs and perfume saw the name Dior reach further than his couture pieces ever could.

While Dior had his own war story – farming, earning for the family and then returning to occupied Paris before liberation – his sister Catherine's was quite different: she joined the Resistance movement against the Germans in 1941. Code-named Caro, she remained active until her arrest by the Gestapo in 1944. She was sent to a French prison and then to a series of camps before escaping in 1945. Little is known of her work because she kept everything secret. Writer Justine Picardie, author of *Miss Dior: A Story of Courage and Couture* (2021), points out that Catherine did not give away a single piece of information to the Gestapo, or following her release. She finally returned to Paris in May 1945 with her beloved big brother waiting for her at the station. Catherine soon took a job at the flower market, and for Christian, his sister became 'part of the imaginary Miss Dior', according to Picardie, the figure 'who represents freedom and love after the ugliness of war'.

In France, Catherine was awarded the Croix de Guerre, the Combatant Volunteer Cross of the Resistance, the Combatant Cross, and was named a Chevalière of the Légion d'honneur, while in the UK, she gained the King's Medal for Courage in the Cause of Freedom. Catherine was Christian's first muse and dedicated herself to growing fields of fragrant roses for Dior Parfum until she died in 2008, at the age of 90.

THE EUGÉNIE DRESS

Voluminous refinement

All fairy-tale froth, the Eugénie is a sweeping blush-pink nylon ball gown from Dior's 1948 autumn/winter collection, Zig Zag. The bell-shaped skirt falls in an *ailée* line, meaning that the hem is longer at the back than the front, and brushes the floor. Soft, horizontal tiers of tulle are stitched close together at the waist, but the space between tiers grows towards the hem, giving a dramatic cascading effect. The bodice is tiny in comparison, sleeveless and smooth (via a little boning magic inside), with a romantic sweetheart neckline and incredibly refined lace details. But it's the skirt that astounds: the voluminous shape, with its hidden architectural structure underneath, seems impossibly light, and the sheerness of the tulle gives the look a misty, ethereal edge. The name seems to invoke France's biggest couture fan from recent history – Empress Eugénie de Montijo, wife of Napoléon III of France, who died in 1920. Despite the dress's fantasy and fullness, fashion critics, on seeing it for the first time, were keen to point out its modern edge too.

THE EVENING ENSEMBLE

Inspired by Greek sculpture

Also part of Dior's 1948 Zig Zag collection was this Evening Ensemble
in off-white silk satin, with pleats and folds that gleam in the light.
The near-iridescent fabric forms a simple bodice, strapless and
sleeveless, with a straight horizontal fold for a neckline. But then Dior
drapes more fabric diagonally across the chest, like a sash, and fixes
the zigzag shape with a dramatic bow. Dior's New Look slim waistline
gives way to a long, slightly flared skirt that gently skims the floor.
Much like the Eugénie gown from the same collection, the whole vibe
is romantic and slightly fantastical, but this time with a sculptural,
Greek goddess edge.

MARLENE DIETRICH

Addicted to Dior

'No Dior, no Dietrich!' said screen legend Marlene Dietrich when negotiating her contracts, or so the story goes. The Hollywood actress adored dressing in Dior, and at the height of her fame was in a position to have her demands met. Back in the 1920s, when she was starting out, she had sung in the nightclubs and bars of Berlin before making her way to the United States in the 1930s, becoming a key performer in Hollywood's glamorous golden age. The German singer and actress was known for her mannish fashion sense, stepping provocatively over gender boundaries, without (it seemed) a care in the world. On screen, she loved to sport men's evening wear, and fashion historians consider her the unofficial inspiration behind Yves Saint Laurent's Le Smoking (a slinky women's tuxedo) while he was head designer at Dior. In photographs and films, Dietrich used her Berlin stage know-how, advising on lighting and poses, and often took her own portraits. And it was Rouge Dior, the house's vibrant red lip colour, that she wore to perfect her look.

The lipstick was made exclusively for Colifichets, aka Ornaments, the tiny in-house boutique tucked under the grand staircase on the ground floor at 30 Avenue Montaigne, and run by Dior's dear friend Carmen Colle. This little treasure-house glittered with Dior creations – silk scarves, baubles and other accessories – and in 1948 Colle suggested that Dior create a ready-to-wear line for the boutique, a reflection of his couture dresses, but simpler and cheaper. This he did, and Rouge Dior lipstick was given to purchasers as a gift. Soon it became the must-have colour, as worn by Marlene Dietrich, and it is still available today, with four 'Couture finishes': satin, matte, metallic and new velvet.

PARIS' FIRST BLACK FASHION MODEL

Dorothea Church

The captivating fashion star of post-war Paris, Dorothea Church had her sister to thank for her ground-breaking couture modelling career. It was Church's sibling, Lois Towles, who encouraged the master's graduate to up sticks for a couple of months and join her on a jaunt to Paris in 1949. Dorothea was already the first Black student at the Dorothy Farrier Charm and Modeling School in Los Angeles, and decided to try modelling in the City of Light on her arrival. Christian Dior hired her on the spot, or so the legend goes. From there, Church modelled for other fashion titans, such as Schiaparelli and Balmain, but it was the House of Dior that gave Dorothea that initial and influential Parisian edge. Within months, Church had gathered a spell-binding wardrobe of couture pieces, and on her return to the United States five years later she began a tour of Black colleges to show off her collection. Eventually, she commandeered a troupe of Black models and became a well-known broadcaster on American radio.

Although Church was popular at the epicentre of the hipster scene in Paris, she undoubtedly encountered prejudice from some in the city. She found it hard to source pieces for Black models to wear in American Black style magazines – in case doing so put off white customers. In Barbara Summers' book *Black and Beautiful* (1998), Church recalled that she borrowed the clothes anyway, and the subsequent shoot for *Ebony*, featuring pieces from Balmain, was a small but significant cultural turning point for young Black fashion fans at the time.

For this illustration, we have dressed Dorothea in Dior's Junon evening gown from his 1949 autumn/winter collection. Rendered in silk gros de Tours (a slightly ribbed silk fabric, like taffeta but with a coarser feel), the gown has layers of silk tulle and skirt flounces cut in the shape of peacock feathers, which are stiffened with horsehair. Intricate peacock blue sequinned and beaded embroidery is on the tip of each 'feather' in an ombré design, and the piece is named in honour of Juno, the Roman goddess of marriage and fertility, herself a fan of the preening bird.

JEAN DAWNAY

Dior's English rose

In a delightful short film for the Victoria and Albert Museum in 2019, Princess Katya Galitzine looks through old black and white fashion shots of her late mother, Christian Dior house model Jean Dawnay. One portrait from *L'Officiel* magazine in a full Dior look has Dawnay 'serene and sophisticated from having been this rather plain English girl,' says Galitzine affectionately, 'and this is who she became'.

During the Second World War, Dawnay had a full and fascinating career, from working in a parachute factory to joining the UK military intelligence network (the Special Operations Executive), codebreaking at Bletchley Park, and working for the Allied forces in Berlin. It was after being demobbed in 1946 that she tried modelling in London. Although she had posed for the eminent photographers Cecil Beaton, John French and Baron, at the age of 24 she decided to try her luck in Paris. Dawnay found herself knocking on the doors of three of the city's most celebrated design houses. All of them offered her work, but Dawnay cleverly chose the designer she thought had the most prestige, even though it paid the least. It was 1949 (the same year that iconic model Dorothea Church arrived in the city), and soon Dawnay became the first well-known English model to work in the salon at Christian Dior.

On her first day in January 1950, she was ushered into Dior's personal studio. 'He was so pleasant and polite to me that it put me to ease immediately,' writes Dawnay in her book, *Model Girl* (1955), 'and looked to my mind more like a country priest than a great dress designer. But I soon discovered behind his gentle and unassuming manner was a very shrewd mind.'

She started as a house mannequin – an in-house fitting model, on hand for the house's artisans (seamstresses, embroiderers and pattern cutters) and for fashion shows – and had a whirlwind year of shows and fittings. Notably, Dawnay appeared in Dior's first official British presentation at the Savoy Hotel in London. Perhaps being back in the city made her homesick because she left her Paris-based role soon afterwards. Nonetheless, she remained good friends with Christian Dior and was something of an ambassador for the fashion house until she died in 2016.

INTRIGUE

The secret fashion show for the British royals

After a 'sumptuous presentation at the Savoy [hotel] in London …
my staff and I found ourselves involved in something like a thriller plot',
wrote Dior in his 1956 autobiography. The couturier's first-ever London
show (starring his 'English rose', Jean Dawnay) was a triumph, but lacked
just one element: royal support. At that time, Great Britain – like France
– was still recovering from war, and most ordinary people were living
under rationing, so it would have seemed insensitive for members of the
Royal Family to be seen at such a frivolous event. But 'these ladies were
all devoured with curiosity to see the "New Look" dresses, of which they
had heard so much', said Dior, and a secret fashion show was arranged
at the French embassy the following day.

'Through … Madame Massigli, wife of the French ambassador
in London … it was arranged for us to show the dresses privately to H.M.,
now the Queen Mother, Princess Margaret, the Duchess of Kent and her
sister Princess Olga of Yugoslavia.' Neither the police nor press had been
warned, and Dior describes how the 'huge ball dresses' were transported
undercover, with the 'tell-tale rustle of material' and 'hasty "shhs"' as the
catwalk show was rehearsed in the embassy, with models incorporating
the court etiquette of leaving the room backwards (so as not to turn their
back on the royals). In the end, the Queen asked the models to be
damned with protocol so she could see the back of each dress.

Ultimately, it was Princess Margaret who fell in love with Dior's
work, so he won the commission to design her 21st birthday dress in 1951.
And in 1954, the British royals underlined their special friendship with
the House of Dior by putting on a charity fashion show for the Red Cross
at Blenheim Palace, with Dior in attendance. Photos and newsreels reveal
attendees crammed into a series of salons, the excitement palpable.

When Elizabeth II died in September 2022, the House of Dior
reminded us that 'In 1947, the young Princess Elizabeth was among the
first to discover the New Look in London, establishing a bond between
Dior and the United Kingdom that has endured ever since.'

ANOTHER STAR

Dior and the Légion d'honneur

The Légion d'honneur is France's highest civilian distinction, and in 1950 it was Christian Dior's moment to receive it. Although the couturier had been in business for more than a decade, his own fashion house had been established for only four years, and he held his first show in the spring of 1947. Receiving the Légion d'honneur so soon shows just how rapidly he achieved creative and commercial success.

There is a single image of the presentation, held at Dior's own Milly-la-Forêt estate, where his beloved converted mill house sat amid famous floral gardens. At the small, dressed-down event, *Le Figaro*'s James de Coquet pinned the famous cross to Dior's lapel, the medal twinkling like a star.

Almost 70 years later, the House of Dior's first female creative director, Maria Grazia Chiuri, was also awarded the Légion d'honneur, this time at a ceremony in the Avenue Montaigne salon in Paris. 'Dior is a Maison that represents femininity,' said Chiuri, 'and for this reason I believe that my commitment is to make women aware of their potential, and I thank the Maison that supports me and gives a voice to women and their work. Their commitment can change the world.'

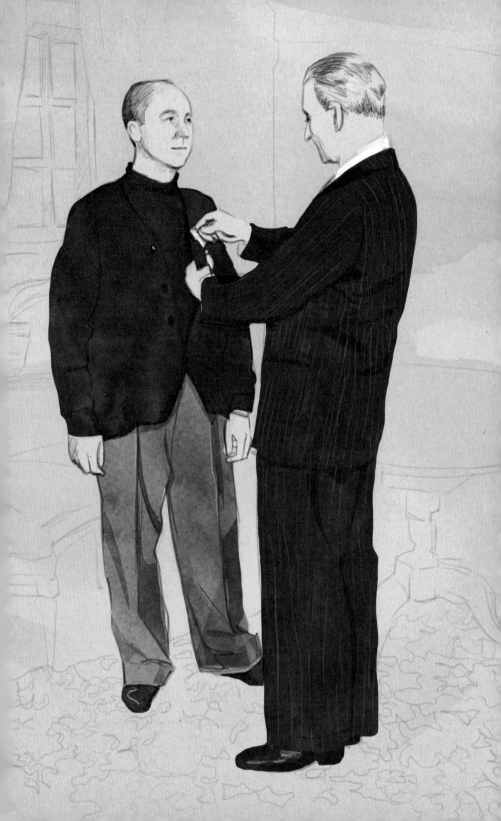

PARTY GIRL

Princess Margaret's 21st birthday dress

'My favourite dress of all,' said HRH Princess Margaret of the Christian Dior gown commissioned for her 21st birthday in 1951. Cecil Beaton took the official portrait of her wearing it, and both dress and image marked not just a coming of age, but a new post-war era for the UK and Europe, one of hope, modernity and the opportunity for a little extravagance.

Beaton's photograph of Margaret and her Dior dress is renowned. She sits on a deep-buttoned pink banquette with an oversized regal painting as backdrop; it's all fairy-tale tones of rose, blood red and gold, and there is Margaret in her off-the-shoulder snowy cream dress. The two-piece outfit has a boned bodice with chiffon sleeves, and an impossibly voluminous, seven-layer skirt with delicate hand embroidery, mother-of-pearl beading and sequins tumbling down to the hem. As fashion legend has it, Dior apparently asked Margaret if she was more a silver or gold person. Of course, she chose gold, and Dior rendered the bodice's front panel with glittering gold rhinestones. The design is a continuation of Dior's New Look, but with a fantastical, mythic vibe, a complete departure from wartime austerity. Dior's occasional use of synthetics, such as rhinestones and sequins, felt modern and daring, tempering the outfit's classic feel. Here was a new princess for a new era.

Margaret had met Christian Dior on her first European excursion in 1949 and the pair had become friends. Dior liked Margaret's sense of style, finding her 'so very charming'. In fact, it was the beginning of a special relationship between Dior and the United Kingdom, with Dior himself an unapologetic Anglophile. There was a concern the country was not ready for Dior's exuberance, but Margaret's 21st birthday dress changed all that.

THE
BRIGHTEST
STAR
BURNS
THE
FASTEST

CHAPTER TWO

(1952–7)

LA CIGALE

A masterpiece of construction

After collections of voluminous skirts and nipped-in waists, Dior
evolved his New Look silhouette with sharper contrasts and colours.
For his 1952 autumn/winter collection, Profile Line, he created La
Cigale, the dramatic femme fatale shape rendered in a weighty, pale grey
moiré fabric that *Harper's Bazaar* noted was 'so heavy it looks like pliant
metal'. Moiré has tonal, iridescent wavy lines reminiscent of cut wood,
and Dior used this effect to highlight the shape. La Cigale is a clever
piece: a series of geometric elements cut and shaped to create a stiff-
seeming dress that *Vogue* described as a 'masterpiece of construction and
execution'. La Cigale (named after the Parisian theatre of the same name,
though the literal meaning, 'cicada', might have alluded to the insect's
stiff carapace) would have seemed incredibly daring as it was paraded
through the salons at 30 Avenue Montaigne – not flowing, sheer and
soft, but somehow firm, structured and sexy. To wear it, the mannequin
had to push the hips forward and hold the stomach in, the bodice
appearing almost moulded to the body. Its modernity places it at the
very height of couture design, although not everyone at the time saw
its chutzpah: *Town & Country* described it merely as a 'day-length
dinner dress'.

THE TULIP
SILHOUETTE

Inspired by nature

Debuted in 1953, the Tulip line was one of Christian Dior's favourites, a further evolution of the New Look. The skirts were still dramatically large, the bust full and the waist nipped in, but Dior made the line more natural. He turned to the tulip (flowers and botanicals were always a go-to for the couturier), and fashion writer Betty Wilson was there to witness the presentation. She described it as 'another new look; not as drastic as the first, but certain to be as far-reaching in its effect. And yet it is so simple – so unpretentious – that it could be worn anywhere, any time.' She also noted the new cut-out necklines, which framed the neck and shoulders, leading 'up to flower-like faces topped by shining, swept-up hair'. Neck framing, said Wilson, 'is the key to the entire Dior silhouette, which forms a tulip flower, then curves down to a tiny waist and stem-straight skirt'. For the evening silhouette, some dresses were covered with 'scales, made of thousands of minute pale pink sequins; others are closely covered with larger scales made of pleated white tulle, each scale outlined with pearls' and formed an inverted tulip flower.

Prints were 'very important and unbelievably lovely. Some show a Chinese influence (big flowering branches on a plain background); others are copied from Persian enamels and are as brilliant as a hummingbird's wings.' The colours astounded the writer; the collection was a beige-free zone: 'No neutral tones. No navy blue. Spring green comes first. Then yellow, vermilion, pale pink, and pale blue.' Wilson loved Dior's accessories; she was so effusive about the umbrellas with their light bamboo handles and thick silk 'the colour of Devonshire cream; in pale champagne or – most desirable of all – that heavenly Dior spring green …' that she may have ordered one in each colour.

PRINCESS GRACE IN DIOR

A love affair with style

Before she fell for a prince, Grace Kelly had already fallen for Dior. The actress wore the Caracas dress from his 1954 spring/summer New York collection to the premiere of Hitchcock's *Rear Window* – and with it, her style credentials were set. Kelly was the sublime female lead in *Rear Window* and was also loved for her style on and off screen. Wearing Dior seemed to signify a thoughtful, intellectual approach to glamour; her star was in the ascendent. But then, aged 26 and at the height of her fame as an actress, Kelly retired from acting and married Prince Rainier III of Monaco.

Although Kelly chose MGM's costume designer Helen Rose to create both her wedding dresses (one for the private civil ceremony, the other for the public event), Dior pieces made up around a third of the star's voluminous wardrobe, and it was Dior she turned to for her first public appearance since the announcement of her engagement. America, it seemed, was about to get its first princess, and all eyes were on Kelly. She chose a special creation by Dior himself for the televised appearance, and later that year appeared in official photographs by Yousuf Karsh wearing Dior's Flamme dress. Later, after Christian Dior died, Kelly became close to his successor, Marc Bohan, making her one of the house's most long-standing and best-known ambassadors. Indeed, she officially opened the first-ever Baby Dior boutique at 28 Avenue Montaigne in 1967 with Bohan by her side.

THE MUGUET DRESS

Incorporating a favourite motif

Christian Dior loved the fragile, fragrant *muguet des bois*, or lily of the valley, which the modern House of Dior describes as 'the symbol of fine weather heralding the arrival of spring and the haute couture season'. Fascinated with fortune-telling, omens and lucky charms, Dior 'would sew a sprig of it into the hem of each of his dresses' and was known to have a posy with him constantly. As a result, prints of the delicate wildflower have been a recurring inspiration for the brand for decades, from couture to perfume, nail colours and homeware.

Although Dior created a lily of the valley dress for actress Françoise Arnoul to wear in the movie *Paris Palace Hotel* in 1956, and his 1957 spring/summer Libre line featured an iconic Muguet dress, in 1954, Dior created a lily of the valley-inspired collection. It included this delicious evening suit: a raglan sleeve jacket and mid-length skirt in rich black satin, trimmed with a velvet and jet fringe. The fitted jacket has a cutaway closure and small, cheeky peplum. The full-length ballerina skirt has loose, unpressed box pleats and thigh-skimming trim. To this day, lily of the valley is gifted to the entire house every 1 May.

RIVER OF FLOWERS

The fashion world mourns

At Christian Dior's funeral on 29 October 1957 there were so many
flowers that a river of them ran through Place de l'Étoile. A throng of
5,000 waited outside the church of Saint-Honoré d'Eylau, and inside
was a star-studded gathering of 2,000 – titans of intellectual thought,
commercial creativity and minor royalty. Writing in the *New York
Times Magazine* in 2002, fashion critic Tim Blanks – in his usual acerbic
manner – likened the death of Dior to Elvis Presley's. Just like the late,
great singer, Dior did indeed die at the height of his fame and, just like
Elvis, he had a lifelong love affair with rich food. He adored classic
cuisine with a Dom Pérignon flourish, a double breakfast and rare
ingredients. 'In other words,' wrote Blanks, 'he liked to eat.' And yet his
death from a heart attack during a trip to Montecatini on 24 October was
completely unexpected. Just a decade after the debut of the New Look,
Dior was dead, and the international fashion community was grieving.

Floral tributes arrived in such numbers that the House of Dior
was granted permission by the City of Paris to lay them out in public.
'The Arc de Triomphe was afloat in a sea of blossom,' wrote Blanks.
'The man himself would have been suitably impressed, given that flowers
were almost the equal of fashion and food in his pantheon of passions.'
The guest list was as impressive as any salon show: 'Jean Cocteau sat
next to the Duchess of Windsor,' said Blanks, and 'Pierre Cardin fainted.'

Blanks pointed out that in 1957, when *Time* magazine featured
Dior on the cover (the first designer to have the honour), he was referred
to as the P.T. Barnum of fashion. But Blanks thought differently, and
looking at the great couturier's life some four decades after his death,
'it brings to mind not Barnum,' he wrote, 'but a gourmandizing dreamer
of another stripe. Yes, indeed, Christian Dior was the Elvis of haute
couture.' This deliciously sharp but somewhat glib depiction of the great
designer hints at the crisis in which the house now found itself. With its
head creative and beloved dream-maker gone, the search for a successor
was put into action before the river of flowers had even started to wilt.
That same day, as the procession entered the church, the eyes of the
house fell on a funeral guest and friend of Dior, a young man named
Yves Saint Laurent.

'IT WAS A NATIONAL EVENT. IT WAS AS IF FRANCE HAD CEASED TO LIVE ... WHEN DIOR'S COFFIN ARRIVED IN THE VAR REGION, WHERE HE WAS BURIED, IT CROSSED THROUGH CITIES AND TOWNS WHERE WOMEN BEARING FLOWERS WERE WAITING.'

Pierre Bergé, friend of Dior

THE
NEW
ERA

CHAPTER THREE

(1957–76)

THE SUCCESSORS

Yves Saint Laurent

'For me, working for Christian Dior was like a miracle had taken place,' wrote Yves Saint Laurent, the one-time 'little prince of fashion', in 1983. 'I had endless admiration for him … He taught me the roots of my art. I owe him a major part of my life, and no matter what happened to me later, I never forgot the years I spent at his side.'

Yves Saint Laurent, the theatrical and theatre-loving show-off of his family, who was bullied at school (like so many other kids who eventually come out as gay), arrived in Paris in 1954 at the age of 18. After less than a year at L'École de la Chambre Syndicale de la Couture Parisienne (the capital's internationally renowned fashion school), and having just turned 19, Saint Laurent dropped out to join Dior as his assistant. Just two years later, following Dior's sudden death, Saint Laurent was named creative director of the house. He was only 21 years old.

The young couturier in waiting had only months to prepare the 1958 spring/summer collection, so he did what he always did in the early days of designing a collection and returned to his hometown of Oran in Algeria to sketch. The images that he usually prepared for Dior were now presented to the house itself, as Saint Laurent was in control. Astoundingly, the grieving young man rose to the occasion, and created over six hundred drawings in 15 days, or so the story goes. He loved theatrical costume and, like Dior, became friends with the writer Jean Cocteau, and designed sets and costumes for the dancer Boris Kochno. He poured this creativity into his first solo debut as Dior's successor, but how well had his mentor prepared him for continuing his legacy? The Trapeze collection was a distinct change of mood: free-spirited and modern, yet refined and delicate – and, more importantly, it was a hit. Saint Laurent let go of Dior's signature nipped-in waist in favour of a more fluid silhouette. Previously, the body was glimpsed in powerfully

Saint Laurent's mark on Dior is undeniable.

effective ways, exaggerated and contrasted, but Saint Laurent's approach was to make the body disappear. What's more, the Trapeze line used less fabric and created a fresh, whimsical look.

Days after his debut, Saint Laurent met French industrialist and fashion-lover Pierre Bergé at a dinner organised by Marie-Louise Bousquet, head of the French edition of *Harper's Bazaar*. There was a glow around Saint Laurent, and Bergé was impressed. They kept in touch.

From 1958 to 1960 Yves Saint Laurent created six collections for the House of Dior, controversially drawing on his own youthful social life from the avant-garde style of Paris intellectuals to the beatniks for his 1960 autumn/winter collection: Souplesse, Légèreté, Vie [Suppleness, Lightness, Life]. He even added that beatnik essential, the black turtleneck, and a crocodile leather jacket debossed with oversized scales. It was about as far away from Dior's romantic, ultra-feminine couture ideals as it could be, and did not find favour with everyone. While not every piece Christian Dior had personally created was a unanimous hit – he received a complaint letter from Idaho, USA, that read 'with your so-called genius, you have succeeded in disfiguring my wife. What will you say if I go and send her over to you?' – this beatnik direction had a few too many critics, the patrons were unsure and the house was uneasy.

But then came the French–Algerian war, and towards the end of 1960 Saint Laurent was conscripted for duty. He was hospitalised with depression soon after, by which time the House of Dior had set its eyes on another creative force. In 1958, it had appointed Marc Bohan as creative director of the London subsidiary, and his talent was shining out. Legend has it that Pierre Bergé delivered the news of Saint Laurent's dismissal, and together the two decided to found their own fashion house, which came about in 1962. Today, Yves Saint Laurent's influence on the House of Dior is celebrated, his avant-garde actions now understood; his playful focus on beatnik style exposed the link between haute couture and street style, which today is an essential ingredient. Saint Laurent's mark on Dior is undeniable.

THE SUCCESSORS

Marc Bohan

It is said that Marc Bohan is the most famous fashion designer you've never heard of. Somehow, the man who commanded the longest reign at the very top of the House of Dior, longer than Christian Dior himself, has a far lower profile than the celebrity designers who came before or after. The truth is, from his first collection as creative director in 1961, Bohan was feverishly popular. Fashion writer Carrie Johnson was there at the beginning and described the hullabaloo surrounding his first Dior show in the *New York Times*: '…this morning the shouting, clapping, surging mob at the press showing caused chaos in the elegant salon,' she wrote. 'M. Bohan was pushed up against the boiserie [oak panelling], kissed, mauled, and congratulated. Chairs were toppled. Champagne glasses were broken. People were knocked down.' To Johnson, Bohan had seemingly gone back to Dior's roots, returning to the 1920s for inspiration. The designs 'underplayed the bosom', and hiplines were dropped to the hips and flared out. Bohan's signature style, known as the Slim Look, helped to typify the willowy silhouette of the 1960s.

In 1958, the House of Dior appointed Marc Bohan as creative director of the London subsidiary, and with the departure of Yves Saint Laurent in 1960, it was announced that Bohan would take his place in Paris. As Johnson wrote, many thought 'M. Bohan would not be able to do it. That he was "too classic a designer, too quiet".' But he gave the house 30 glittering years, navigating and setting the style of the 1960s and 1970s, expanding the brand and becoming friends with the likes of Elizabeth Taylor, the Duchess of Windsor, Bianca Jagger, Barbra Streisand, Maria Callas and Princess Grace of Monaco. Little wonder that Dior became one of the most powerful fashion houses in the world.

Bohan's signature style, known as the Slim Look, helped to typify the willowy silhouette of the 1960s.

Born in Paris in 1926 to a milliner mother, Bohan worked as a designer for Robert Piguet in 1945, became assistant to British designer Edward Molyneaux in 1949, produced his own eponymous collection in 1953, and was a designer for Jean Patou in 1954. He then joined the House of Dior in 1958 (something of an insurance policy against Saint Laurent). His debut collection in Paris certainly helped to steady the house, reigniting its patrons' passions; this was the Dior they knew.

Bohan became known for his elegant simplicity, his love of abstract art and his celebrity clientele. But why has his legacy been overlooked? Perhaps it was something to do with the apparently temporary nature of his appointment; in 2007, when Bohan had been with the house for nearly five decades, *Women's Wear Daily* reported that he was only ever meant to be a stand-in, a trusted and talented place-holder, until a permanent designer could be found. Or perhaps it is something to do with the industry itself; coinciding with the arrival of Bohan, couture had started to change, youth fashion was developing and the golden age of haute seemed to be over. Dior collections would set a trend that in turn inspired garment-makers and retailers to create similar pieces at a lower cost. But the 1960s disdained all that; young women turned away from couture and were instead tantalised by new, ready-to-wear designs made just for them. No longer did couture so easily set the trend, and Bohan's House of Dior needed to change. Luckily, he was just the man to do it.

BOHAN'S DEBUT LOOK

The Green Park day dress

Marc Bohan told *Women's Wear Daily* in 2007 of the atmosphere in which he launched his vision for the great couture house. 'Before my first collection for Dior,' he said, 'most people had the knives out … People were licking their lips. They were waiting for me to fall on my face.' But some writers, such as Carrie Johnson of the *New York Times*, declared it a sure-fire hit. Known as Charme 62, this haute couture autumn/winter collection offered a supple and slim silhouette: 'the shoulders are natural, the waist undulates, the hips are very flat,' said the press release. One short, flared and ruffled wool look, the Green Park day dress, seemed to embody the era – even now, the piece clearly reads as 1960s. It was originally shown in green but was soon commissioned by a patron who asked for the piece to be rendered in bright scarlet, accidentally creating an icon. The scarlet long-sleeved version is regal but fresh and playful. Bohan had somehow achieved what Yves Saint Laurent did not: evolving the brand with the times but not in such a way as to scare the horses – namely, Dior's patrons.

THE OSCAR DRESS

Elizabeth Taylor

Elizabeth Taylor's first Oscar dress, with its lemon-yellow chiffon bodice and kooky buttermilk bubble skirt in silk faille, lively green taffeta belt and embroidered silk flowers and bees, was long thought to be lost – or at least locked in an archive gathering dust. The outfit from Marc Bohan's 1961 spring/summer haute couture collection was Taylor's lucky charm at the 33rd Academy Awards. She won an Oscar for her performance in *Butterfield 8*, a blighted production during which she contracted pneumonia. The award helped her to recover from the negative publicity provoked by an alleged affair with a married member of the *Butterfield* cast.

The lost dress was eventually discovered in an old suitcase belonging to Anne Sanz, the wife of a former bodyguard, chauffeur and friend to Taylor and her then husband Richard Burton. It was auctioned in 2022 for more than £60,000, the rather high price tag being a nod to the dress's notoriety. Taylor had twice been passed over for an Oscar, so it seemed that a little Dior magic brought her luck that night. Footage from the event shows a delightfully stunned Taylor, white gloved hands held up to her face in shock as she hears she has won. She melts with pleasure before making her way to the podium to give a breathless acceptance speech. Taylor carried that lucky dress with her for a decade before handing it over to Sanz.

THE TUNIC DRESS

Easy to wear yet sophisticated

'I'm not designing to please myself or for a photograph,' Marc Bohan said in 1988 in an interview with *USA Today*. 'I am designing for a woman who wants to look her best. I have always in mind the reaction of women I know.' With this singular focus, Bohan stayed away from Christian Dior's structural and theatrical showpieces and instead focused on creating clothing that women wanted to wear. This embroidered Tunic dress from Dior's 1966 spring/summer haute couture collection is rendered in cotton with metal, glass and plastic, and is a perfect example of Bohan's easy and refined approach to style. The beadwork, a seemingly haphazard arrangement, is a nod to Bohan's love of abstract art. It's pure 1960s style.

'MY AIM IS TO
MAKE CLOTHES
THAT ARE
SOPHISTICATED
IN THEIR
SIMPLICITY, WITH
A TOUCH OF
CHEEKINESS
NOW AND THEN.'

Marc Bohan

THE BAYADÈRE DRESS

Princess Grace in full colour

Although she had given her heart to Christian Dior, Princess Grace of Monaco was a lifelong fan of the fashion house, whomever was at the helm. She memorably wore Marc Bohan's Technicolor Bayadère dress, part of his 1967 haute couture spring/summer collection, and named after the fantastical classic ballet set in ancient India. Although bias-cut skirts and drop-waist dresses were the core of Bohan's style, the Bayadère dress was flowing and dramatic. Its vivid yellow and orange chiffon glowed with colour arranged in geometric chevrons, and Princess Grace wore it with gold cuffs and a neckpiece studded with stones. She wasn't the only celebrity to acquire the colourful dress: it was also worn by actress Olivia de Havilland, and later Princess Grace's daughters, Caroline (for whom Bohan created a wedding dress in the 1980s) and Stephanie, who became fans of his work.

'A TOUCH OF CHEEKINESS'

Sophia Loren in Dior

'An X certificate,' reported fashion writer Felicity Green in the *Daily Mirror* in 1965. 'That's what I'd give Marc Bohan's show at Dior today. Strictly grown-up – for the over-sixteens only – Bohan's collection is strong stuff and will, I predict, be a winner.' It was his relationship with the youthquake fashions sweeping through the 1960s that Green was interested in; Bohan had to balance the zeitgeist of the fresh, new and modern with the tradition of couture and its naturally older, more affluent customer. The writer also predicted that Bohan would become 'a bosom pal to all those neglected ladies of a certain age who don't look their best in thigh-high plastic macs and matching boots'.

Although she looked good in anything and everything, it was Sophia Loren to whom Bohan became a 'bosom pal'. It was the Bohan-led House of Dior that Loren turned to for her costumes in the 1966 spy thriller *Arabesque* with Gregory Peck. The clothes are otherworldly and, interestingly, Loren looks amazing wearing just what Green had critiqued – a bright red plastic mac and high black boots. This hooded haute couture creation shows that the actress never took herself too seriously; she had a true affinity with Bohan's 'touch of cheekiness'.

THE
POWER
HOUSE

CHAPTER FOUR

(1976–96)

LISA TAYLOR

'Fetching Is Your Dior'

In the mid-1970s and early 1980s, the House of Dior repositioned itself for the coming age of brash consumerism, sexualised glamour and the diamond-dripping moneyed elite. For the advertising campaign that would help with that repositioning, the house employed radical wunderkind photographer Chris von Wangenheim, model Lisa Taylor and a toothy Dobermann to create an iconic set of images.

Born in Germany, von Wangenheim moved to New York City at the age of 23 and worked as a photographer's assistant for David Thorpe and James Moore. He soon started his own studio and shot mainly for *Vogue*, but also *Harper's Bazaar*, *Interview* and *Playboy*. His take on high fashion was less reverent and more provocative than that of other photographers at the time, with jarring and glossy set pieces and a strange sense of foreboding. 'I realized that getting my picture was more important to me than the discomfort of someone not understanding, or someone's opposition to my goals,' he once said.

For the advertising shoot 'Fetching Is Your Dior', his photographs of Lisa Taylor show her canine friend apparently biting her wrist, which was glittering with diamonds, and the image is perhaps one of the most memorable of the era. Von Wangenheim died in a car crash at the age of 39, but his taboo-breaking work continues to have an outsized influence on modern-day image-makers.

DISCO QUEEN

Lauren Hutton

The model-turned-actress Lauren Hutton had played a leading role in *American Gigolo* in 1980, but it was in the French comedy *Tout Feu Tout Flamme*, aka *All Fired Up* (1982), that Hutton's most iconic cinematic look was seen. Marc Bohan was commissioned to make exclusive dresses for both Hutton and her co-star Isabelle Adjani; the latter was given a strapless ball gown, but for Hutton's character the couturier created the ultimate disco dress. It had an impossibly low neckline and was rendered in shimmering, micro-pleated gold lamé. The movie may have been somewhat forgotten, but Bohan's outfit and Hutton's magnetism seemed to ready the House of Dior for a new era, and just one year later, Bohan was awarded the Golden Thimble, the Oscar of haute couture.

In 2014, in a conversation on stage in New York City with fashion expert Fern Mallis, Lauren Hutton described how she first came to model for Dior. 'I was looking through wanted ads,' said Hutton, 'and then [my friend] Arnie said, "Look at this. It says 'Model wanted. Christian Dior. New York. Must have experience.'" I said, "I don't have experience." He said, "Of course you do." I learned my first great New York lesson: lie.'

DIOR'S IDEAL WOMAN

Kelly LeBrock

'Don't hate me because I'm beautiful,' said model and actress Kelly LeBrock in her famous Pantene shampoo commercial. The line became a pop culture catchphrase, and although often lampooned, it seemed the public did just what she asked. LeBrock was a successful model and comic actress, with a special relationship – and lucrative contract – with the House of Dior. Her career started in New York with a 24-page fashion story in *Vogue* when she was just 19 years old. This brought her to the attention of the house, who soon signed her up to work for the brand 30 days a year.

LeBrock played on her 'ideal woman' persona, undercutting it with comic roles in movies such as *The Woman in Red* (1984) and *Weird Science* (1985), and was the perfect 1980s celebrity to focus attention on one of Dior's most controversial lines: the haute fourrure (fur collection). In Richard Avedon-shot advertising images, LeBrock plays a glamorous, moneyed New York socialite smothered in furs. From a contemporary perspective, it's problematic to say the least, but it is a captivating campaign and completely of its time.

OBJECT OF DESIRE

Poison

By the mid-1980s, the House of Dior had already created several delightful signature scents, most of which, like Miss Dior, are still going strong today. But in 1985, Dior released a new fragrance unlike any other. Called Poison, it was sold in a bottle shaped like Snow White's apple, and its rich, seductive berry notes embodied the glamour of the 1980s. It was created by Jean Guichard of the Swiss fragrance and flavour powerhouse Givaudan, under whose auspices he also created 1987's Loulou by Cacharel. Poison was launched at a special celebration with the French actress Isabelle Adjani in attendance.

Today, Dior describes Poison as 'a sultry elixir … born legendary' and the 'ultimate fragrant weapon by Dior for heightened seduction'. Guichard has, in the past, pointed out its place in the top tier of timeless fragrances. In 2014, he told *Time* magazine that students training to be Givaudan noses work from the classics, especially Robert Piguet's Fracas. 'Just as Picasso could not have existed without Van Gogh,' says Guichard, 'without Fracas, there would be no Chloé, no Michael Kors, no Poison by Dior. Fracas is the mother to modern perfume.' Poison has notes of coriander, tuberose and opoponax, a tree gum from the Middle East, and like all the best fragrances, its uniqueness and sheer potency can be divisive.

POISON

Dior

'MARC BOHAN LEFT AN INCALCULABLE LEGACY FOR MAISON DIOR.'

Bianca Jagger

THE BIRTHDAY PARTY

Celebrating four decades

In 1987 there was cause to celebrate: it was the 40th anniversary of the House of Dior, and Marc Bohan's collection felt celebratory, with party dresses that had an exuberant 1980s feel. President François Mitterrand opened the first of many receptions at a large retrospective at the Musée des Arts Décoratifs in Paris, followed by a 500-seat 'glittering black-tie dinner' at 30 Avenue Montaigne. Among those attending, reported the *New York Times*, were Princess Caroline of Monaco, Joan Collins and Jean-Paul Belmondo, with 'Johnny Mathis and Michel Legrand ... to entertain after dinner'.

The subsequent 1987 haute couture spring/summer collection was shown in the courtyard of the Louvre. To the strains of A-ha's *Take On Me*, it opened with a classic New Look outfit, followed by Bohan's party girls clad in ruffled ra-ra skirts, polka dots and impossibly large hats.

BOHAN'S FINALE

Supermodel Iman steps out

Although Iman had walked in Dior shows since 1979, she, like most other people, would not have known that the 1989 haute couture spring/ summer and autumn/winter shows in Paris were to be Marc Bohan's final collections for the house. They were her final shows too, as she retired from modelling that same year. Bohan, captured on video backstage, had won his second Golden Thimble award the year before, and predicted that 1990s style would be 'softer, less aggressive, more feminine'. He would go on to try to harness that spirit at Hartnell, a long-established couture house in London, but sadly, that venture failed. Perhaps Iman saw power in both her and Bohan's departure from the business: 'I believe in one gimmick,' she told British *Vogue* in 2019. 'There is power in a little bit of mystery. Keep a little bit to yourself. Let them want more.'

THE SUCCESSORS

Gianfranco Ferré

In 1989, the eve of a new decade, the House of Dior, 'driven by a postmodern vision of fashion', replaced Marc Bohan with Italian designer and architecture graduate Gianfranco Ferré. The impulse to change direction actually began back in 1984, when Bernard Arnault, owner of Louis Vuitton, purchased Dior and set about developing it and supercharging its brand power. Today, Louis Vuitton accounts for half the profits of Arnault's family-run LVMH mega-company, but Dior was his first acquisition (bought after a tip from a New York cab driver, or so fashion legend goes) and is perhaps the emotional heart of Arnault's empire.

'When I arrived at this prestigious house,' said Ferré in 1995, 'I wanted to respect the Dior style, with fitted silhouettes, large bows, a profusion of organza. I had to pay homage.' Pierre Bergé, then Saint Laurent's chairman, protested: 'I don't think opening the doors to a foreigner – and an Italian – is respecting the spirit of creativity in France,' he declared, but Arnault held firm and, unlike Bohan, whose name had always been somewhat hidden from view, Ferré's soon went on the collection programmes.

Although Ferré obeyed the 'Dior code', the house noted that he gave haute couture a new lease of life 'through the architectural elegance of his suits and the opulence of grand evening dresses'. Although he was known as 'the Frank Lloyd Wright of fashion', he was more like the industry's friendly besuited bear – the opposite of Bohan's slim form – and wore nothing less than a full three-piece suit every day. Like his two Dior predecessors, Ferré drew inspiration from art, and was timely with it: the palette of Paul Cézanne powered his 1995–6 haute couture autumn/winter collection, coinciding with a huge Cézanne retrospective in Paris.

Shown in the garden of the Hôtel Salomon de Rothschild, Ferré's debut Dior collection in 1989 was a success, winning him wide acclaim and the Golden Thimble award, but he found it hard to consistently give the house what it needed. 'Gianfranco Ferré has been trying for a year to give Christian Dior a new image,' wrote Bernadine Morris in the *New York Times* in 1990. 'This time he gave it the most sophisticated position in the current fashion line-up.' And in 1996, at the end of his tenure, Constance C.R. White wrote – again in the *New York Times* – that 'Every eye, it seemed, was dry at the fare-thee-well collection of Gianfranco Ferré for the house of Christian Dior,' and that the designer brought 'the Ferré era at Dior sputtering to a close'.

At college, Ferré made jewellery and trinkets for friends, and his work was soon spotted by the owner of a Milan boutique. His accessories subsequently went on to delight fashion editors Anna Piaggi and Anna Riva. Fashion mogul Walter Albini encouraged Ferré to move into design, and the young man was suddenly – and perhaps accidentally – the next thing in fashion. Ferré worked in India for an Italian brand and freelanced before setting up his own brand and finally his own design house in 1978. After his Dior appointment, Ferré cleverly kept his own brand alive (although he closed his own couture department), and produced the audience-pleasing showpieces and a ready-to-wear line for the great House of Dior until 1996.

For his 1992 haute couture spring/summer collection, Ferré revealed his most iconic Dior look, the Palladio dress. The long, pleated white silk georgette-crepe dress looked just like a Palladian column, the embroidery giving a *trompe l'oeil* effect. The dress has its own surprising fan base within the anime community, as it is thought to be the inspiration for Princess Serenity's dress in *Sailor Moon*.

After his departure from the great French fashion house, Ferré returned to his own hugely successful house, added a denim line and opened new stores, proving that there is life after Dior.

LADY DIOR

Princess Diana and Dior's It Bag

Without the help of Bernadette Chirac, would the Lady Dior bag – now one the house's most celebrated accessories – be as iconic as it is today? The First Lady of France presented the tiny black leather bag, with its signature Dior quilting (an echo of the Napoleon III chairs set out for Dior shows), to Princess Diana for jointly opening a 1995 Cézanne exhibition at the Grand Palais.

Designed by Gianfranco Ferré, the 'Chouchou', as the bag was then known, was allegedly made the night before the event – with Dior's craftspeople scrambling to assemble 140 pieces of lambskin leather with Dior *cannage* (geometric) top stitching and four golden Dior letters. By 1996, after accruing a little Diana magic, the bag was officially renamed, and the Lady Dior bag became one of the world's most wanted accessories.

HIGH
DRAMA

CHAPTER FIVE

(1996–2006)

THE SUCCESSORS

John Galliano

It was out with Ferré and in with fashion's bad boy, John Galliano. To this day, there are few designers as dramatic and extravagant, and Galliano lived up to his reputation for the extraordinary, from his much-fabled debut collection in 1996 to his troubled departure in 2011. The House of Dior remembers Galliano as the 'British designer with a rock 'n' roll spirit' and credits him (and his chaotic energy) with reinventing the Dior haute couture tradition 'by fusing it with his dreamlike imagination'. Under Galliano, Dior shows became breathtaking theatrical extravaganzas, powered by supermodels, celebrities and the designer's 'spectacular scenography'. This was fashion as spectacle, and Galliano helped Dior to soar.

Born in Gibraltar in 1960, Galliano was Britain's brash upstart, the Central Saint Martins art-school kid who graduated in 1984 into a London mired in a hotchpotch of competing styles – New Romantics, Buffalo, Goth and Rave – all rubbing shoulders at artful nightspots, such as the infamous weekly Taboo club night. 'I met John … at the show he put on to graduate from art school in London,' DJ Jeremy Healy (one of Galliano's closest friends) told Michael Specter in a *New Yorker* article. 'My girlfriend was modelling, and when she walked down the runway she had a tree branch coming out of her head and she was waving a dead mackerel. An actual dead fish. The whole show was like that. It takes a lot to shock me. But I just thought, what the hell is this bloke up to?'

Galliano's Dior is remembered for his bias-cut dresses, his 2004 haute couture spring/summer collection dominated by queens and pharaohs ... his iconic Saddle Bag and for what he got away with.

London boutique Browns purchased Galliano's fishy graduate collection, and the designer bravely set up his own eponymous brand. When the project failed financially in 1989, Galliano decamped to Paris, living the somewhat rootless existence Christian Dior had initially experienced. With the help of American *Vogue* editor-in-chief Anna Wintour and editor-at-large André Leon Talley, he eventually secured more funding and continued to build his own brand.

If the finances were hard won, the buzz around Galliano only grew. 'In the early 90s,' Dana Thomas wrote in the *New York Times Style Magazine* in 1999, 'Galliano used to live with three or four other guys in a flat ... Those were the days when Galliano was known as much for his party antics as for his witty design, when he lost backers like baby teeth and had a hard time keeping an apartment lease, when he'd sleep on friends' sofas and floors.' But his imperilled 1993 spring/summer show was a masterpiece, and in 1995, Bernard Arnault appointed Galliano as head designer at Givenchy (making him the first British designer to head up a French couture house). Just one year later, he replaced Gianfranco Ferré at the House of Dior.

His Dior debut, the 1997 haute couture spring/summer collection, harnessed the full power of the house's skilled artisans, who sat backstage at the show to see their work in action. He also maximised Dior's celebrity connections, although Galliano waited another collection or so before stretching the house's appetite for spectacle.

Today, Galliano's Dior is remembered for his bias-cut dresses, his 2004 haute couture spring/summer collection dominated by queens and pharaohs (inspired by a visit to Egypt the year before), his iconic Saddle Bag and for what he got away with. 'Today, designers would be crucified for putting models in newspaper dresses and calling it a Hobo collection,' writes Daniel Rodgers in *Dazed* magazine, 'but Galliano came under little scrutiny for his [2000 spring/summer] show, which had been inspired by the unhoused Parisians he encountered on his daily jogs … [in which] threadbare outfits were accessorised with (empty) bottles of liquor and dangling trash.' Fascinatingly, the *Zoolander* movie, which parodies the fashion industry, was released just one year later and begs the question: did Galliano's Hobo show inspire the movie's 'Derelicte' collection, or vice versa?

At Dior, Galliano's star rose and rose until 2011, when he suddenly fell 'from the highest echelons of the fashion establishment', wrote the media company *Business of Fashion*. A Paris court gave Galliano a suspended fine of €6,000 for anti-Semitic 'public insults' caught on video outside La Perle, a gay bar in the Marais district, and he was fired soon afterwards. For a moment, it seemed both Dior and Galliano would never recover, but what a difference a couple of years makes. Galliano moved to Maison Martin Margiela in 2014, and Dior went on to announce its next creative director in 2012.

'STYLE IS WEARING
AN EVENING DRESS
TO McDONALD'S,
WEARING HEELS
TO PLAY FOOTBALL.
IT IS PERSONALITY,
CONFIDENCE
AND SEDUCTION.'

John Galliano

THE SLIP DRESS
Princess Diana at the Met

In 1996 the House of Dior celebrated its 50th anniversary, which was marked by a grand exhibition organised by the Costume Institute at the Metropolitan Museum of Art in New York. At the launch party, Princess Diana wore a lingerie-like, sapphire blue silk gown, a Galliano creation from his first-ever Dior collection, and carried a Lady Dior bag by Gianfranco Ferré. To accompany her outfit, Diana wore some of her most striking jewels, including a multi-strand pearl choker to which was attached a huge sapphire brooch surrounded with a double row of diamonds. They made Galliano's slip of a dress stunningly glamorous.

GALLIANO'S BFF

Naomi Campbell

For his 1997 Dior haute couture autumn/winter collection Galliano dressed the British supermodel Naomi Campbell as an Indian-style dancing girl. The outfit – a gold lamé bra and tiny sarong skirt – is a riot of artisanal embellishments, including arabesque, moon and butterfly embroideries, a ruff-like neckpiece, bracelets, feathers, tassels, fringes and strands of beads.

It was Campbell who helped Galliano book a place at a rehab centre in Arizona, where he spent six weeks undergoing treatment following his departure from Dior. 'At first alcohol was like a crutch outside of Dior,' Galliano told Ingrid Sischy in *Vanity Fair* in 2013. 'Then I would use it to crash after the collections … and then I was a slave to it. Then the pills kicked in because I couldn't sleep. Then the other pills kicked in because I couldn't stop shaking.' In *The Super Models* documentary series for Apple TV+ (2023), Campbell opens up about her own alcohol and drug problems between 1998 and 2005; she was perfectly positioned to help her friend, and she did just that.

THE BEAUTIFULLY UGLY DRESS

Nicole Kidman at the 1997 Oscars

'Nicole! Come tell me why you wore such an ugly colour!' screeched the late, great Joan Rivers across the red carpet at the 69th Academy Awards in 1997. Her prey was Oscar-winner Nicole Kidman, and the dress – a Dior chartreuse gown by Galliano – was a heart-stopper. It was all part of Rivers' schtick, of course; she was booked to churn out acidic one-liners about the celebrities' outfits, but her take-down of Kidman's look was lip-bitingly embarrassing. 'John [Galliano] made it for me, and I love it,' Kidman countered to *Women's Wear Daily* on the day. 'I don't know if people will get it. But if they don't, well maybe they should.' The dress – and Kidman's look – is now considered one of the most memorable and best-loved Oscar fashion moments.

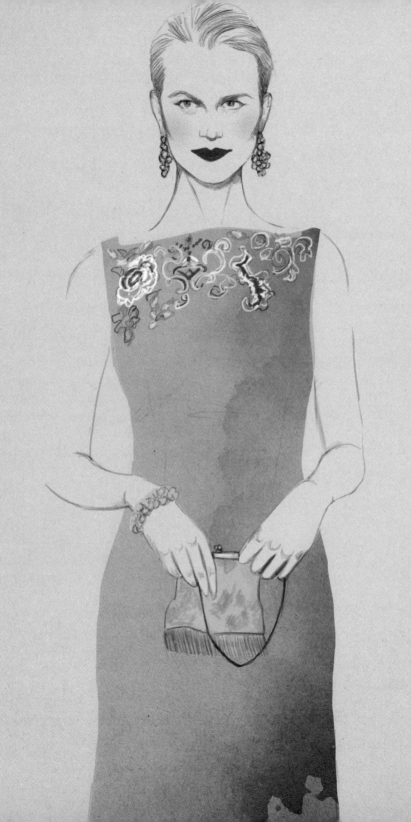

OBJECT OF DESIRE

The Dior Saddle Bag

John Galliano's Saddle Bag was the ultimate must-have accessory in the early 2000s, the heyday for fashion It Bags. Its ugly-chic aesthetic – a shrunken saddle shape with a massive 'D' for Dior dangling like a stirrup – is said to have been inspired by Helmut Newton's iconic and fetish-edged image *Saddle I*, Paris 1976. The House of Dior's accessory line debuted in 1999, and sales had jumped up 60 per cent the year after the bag was released. Everybody had one, from Paris Hilton, Nicole Ritchie, Christina Aguilera and Mischa Barton to Sarah Jessica Parker's Carrie Bradshaw in *Sex and the City*. But just like the Beanie Baby craze of the mid-1990s, the Saddle Bag's white-hot popularity peaked and then plummeted, going from numinous to naff, and it was conspicuously absent from Dior's spring/summer ready-to-wear shows in 2007.

Since then, the Saddle Bag has made a slow but assured comeback, powered by vintage reselling apps and celebrity aficionados. In fact, at Maria Grazia Chiuri's 2018 autumn/winter show, it made its official comeback (slightly enlarged to carry a smartphone) in Dior's once brash-seeming logo print. Fashion fans can again saddle up and ride it home.

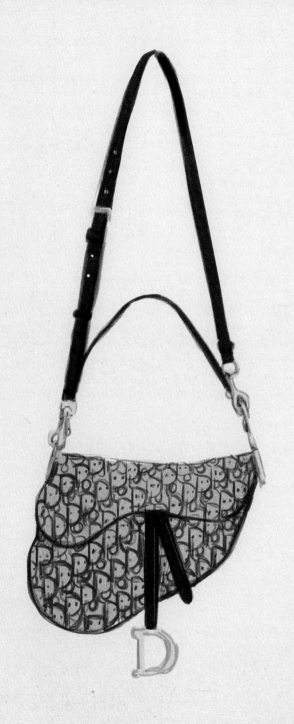

OBJECT OF DESIRE

J'Adore Dior

J'Adore Dior is perhaps the best example of an enduring link between a fragrance and the celebrity who fronts it. Think of the shimmering, golden-hued advertising campaign and the image of a statuesque Charlize Theron will spring into your mind. 'As the face of the fragrance for almost 20 years,' writes Jennifer George in *Harper's Bazaar*, 'Theron seems as timeless and elegant as what's inside the bottle, a scent that has stood the test of time since its launch in 1999.'

Created by Calice Becker, the director of Givaudan's perfumery school, the fragrance is her fantastical imagining of what gold might smell like. Its fresh and floral vibe uses jasmine, Christian Dior's favourite lily of the valley, and tuberose, with melon and mandarin notes and a little musk as its foundation. It launched with Estonian model Carmen Kass as its first ambassador and speedily became a top seller.

JOKER IN THE PACK

Celine Dion at the Oscars

Among all the glittering stars attending the 71st Academy Awards in Los Angeles in 1999, it should perhaps have been Gwyneth Paltrow's night. She won best leading actress for the historical romcom *Shakespeare in Love,* and the movie itself won a slew of awards, including best picture. But fashion fans tend to remember someone else, another celebrity, whose outfit stole the show – the Canadian singer Celine Dion in a brilliant white Dior creation. At the time, it was thought of as a misfire, with Ms Dion hitting the headlines for all the wrong reasons. In that peak gossip blog era, the comments were merciless, apparently paving the way for the social media trolls of decades to come. Critics had a field day.

Topping any number of worst-dressed lists, Dion's outfit – a beautifully cut white jacket and voluminous trousers – seemed innocuous enough, only she elected to wear the Galliano creation … backwards. Styled with a cocked white fedora, diamanté-encrusted Ray-Bans and an enigmatic smile, the outfit confounded everyone. The backwards tux jacket became the last word in bad celeb style and was even (affectionately) lampooned in the opening credit sequence of cult Australian comedy series *Kath & Kim.*

Over the years, though, the unforgettable outfit has shifted in our collective perception. Its daring, slightly comic edge now seems transgressive rather than a fashion faux pas. Perhaps this is something to do with the enduring star power of Dion herself, her cult following, endless memes, refreshingly offbeat style and camp depiction in off-Broadway musical *Titanique.* 'When I wore that look … everyone was wearing dresses, not pants,' Dion told *People* magazine in 2017. 'I was the only one with pants in a backward suit from Galliano, and if I [did] this today it would work. It was avant-garde at the time.' Sometimes fashion doesn't have to be serious; Celine Dion got the joke decades before the rest of us.

DIOR HOMME

Hedi Slimane

In 2000, the House of Dior said bonjour to lanky Parisian maverick Hedi Slimane, the creative head of Dior Homme until 2007. From the beginning, Slimane exuded that indefinable French cool, and his personal style – threadbare vintage band T-shirts, skinny jeans (novel at the time) and a worn leather biker jacket – seemed to permeate his work.

After studying history of art at L'École du Louvre and assisting Jean-Jacques Picart with an exhibition for Louis Vuitton, Slimane had earned a place among insouciant Paris trendsetters. But in 1996, with no training and little experience, it was a surprise to most that he was hired as Yves Saint Laurent's ready-to-wear menswear director by Pierre Bergé. Although it was at Saint Laurent that Slimane developed his trademark style, and his 2000-01 autumn/winter Black Tie collection was a hit, it was Dior Homme (DH) where he would transform men's style. His first DH collection proffered a menswear style that was skinny and seductive, with an ambiguous sexuality, a viewpoint that loitered at the intersection of indie rock, Berlin electro and modern art.

It was Marc Bohan who first created Dior menswear, founding the Christian Dior Monsieur line in 1969. It was then overseen by Christian Benais, followed by Gérard Penneroux in 1980, Dominique Morlotti in 1983 and Patrick Lavoix in 1992 ahead of Slimane's appointment. By April 2002, he had won the CFDA (Council of Fashion Designers of America) International Designer award – the first menswear designer to receive it – and it was presented to him by the singer David Bowie, whom Slimane dressed for his tours.

Slimane seemed to use thin, grungy boys on his catwalks and in ad campaigns, street-casting skaters and oddballs.

From a contemporary viewpoint, Slimane's clothes were not for every man – certainly not for the athletic or the cake-inclined. Instead, his pieces were clearly cut for spindly men like himself. 'Well, there came this new line from Hedi Slimane at Dior that you needed to be slim to wear,' said Karl Lagerfeld. 'It said: "You want this? Go back to your bones." And so … I lost 88 pounds and never got them back.' Slimane seemed to use thin, grungy boys on his catwalks and in ad campaigns, street-casting skaters and oddballs, and seemed to outdo himself each collection with even thinner and grungier discoveries.

An accomplished photographer too, Slimane published photo books, and also made stage outfits for performers such as Mick Jagger, Jack White, Franz Ferdinand and The Kills. Razorlight (remember them?) recorded a special song, 'In the Morning', for the 2006 Dior Homme autumn/winter show, and Slimane even had his own blog. He was at the epicentre of a cultural movement he helped create; the style of his skinny and stylish goth-edged friends writ large. Like the showmen who had, in part, inspired Slimane's Dior Homme designs, he departed the house of his own accord in 2006, leaving them wanting more.

DIOR HAUTE COUTURE

Oriental influences

'Before I visited China,' Galliano told the Metropolitan Gallery's Andrew Bolton in 2015, 'it was the fantasy that drew me to it, the sense of danger and mystery conveyed through Hollywood. Much later, I learned more about the real China through research – paintings, literature, architecture … But, yes, my initial interest in China was fuelled by movies, by their fantasized and romanticized portrayals.'

Galliano's 2003 haute couture spring/summer collection for Dior drew its inspiration from China and Japan, and offered up one of his most theatrical stagings. What impressed – indeed, wowed – was the designer's maximalist take on just about everything. 'In Galliano's hands, the vivid colors and patterns of Chinese costume and Japanese kimonos got transformed into some of the *hugest* clothes ever invented,' wrote *Vogue*'s Sarah Mower. 'Models, almost completely submerged in cocooning swaths of brocade, taffeta and exploding chiffon flounces, teetered along on vertiginous platforms.'

REESE WITHERSPOON

1957 Dior dress at the 2006 Oscars

'I have fallen in love with so many costumes over the years,' said
Reese Witherspoon in 2020, 'and I keep one from every movie. But one
special dress stands out. My Oscar dress in 2006: it was a 1957 Christian
Dior bought at a vintage store in Paris. So dreamy!' The night she won
the Oscar for her performance as June Carter Cash in *Walk the Line*,
Witherspoon wore a vintage beaded dress from the House of Dior,
created in the 1950s (some date the dress to 1955). Not everyone loved
the look: Jess Cartner-Morley in the *Guardian*, for example, called it
'more toilet-roll dolly than Hollywood icon. It drowns her tiny frame
and takes the Southern sweetheart persona into overkill ... Dolly Parton
could add sleeves and wear this next year.'

60 YEARS OF DIOR

Supermodels assemble

Linda, Naomi, Helena, Karen, Amber and Shalom … For Dior's 60th birthday extravaganza in 2007, Galliano assembled a power pack of early 1990s supermodels for what might have been the celebration of the decade. He filled the catwalk with famous faces and dressed them in gorgeous geisha-inspired gowns. But Galliano's show ended with a slightly melancholy feeling. The house's early period was the show's starting point, with Gisele Bündchen in a Bar Suit and Raquel Zimmermann in a pale cream, circle-skirted dress, but Puccini's tragic opera *Madame Butterfly* was the end point, with rich embroidered satin, origami detailing and Galliano's go-to, chiffon.

There was no doubt that Galliano focused on the artists and illustrators who had influenced Christian Dior, and 'The underlying mood was of respectful homage to two men who devoted their lives to fashion and died too young,' wrote Sarah Mower in *Vogue*. 'Christian Dior himself and Galliano's chief designer, Steven Robinson, who tragically passed away … while working toward this collection.' Noting the rarefied production process and eye-watering cost of couture, the *Guardian*'s Jess Cartner-Morley had a prediction: 'It is a very romantic world of heart-stopping young beauties dressed in chiffon; it is also, in today's ruthless financial climate, probably heading for a tragic end.'

THE
VELVET
ROPE

CHAPTER SIX

(2007–2016)

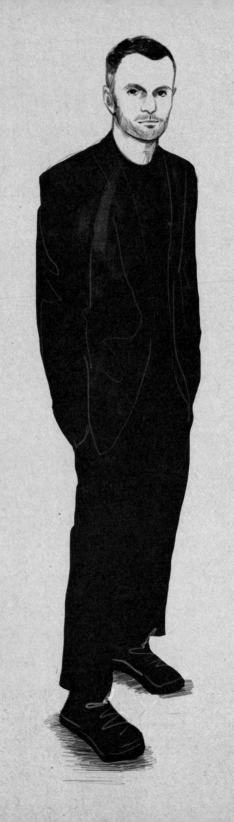

DIOR HOMME

Kris Van Assche

Belgian designer Kris Van Assche took over from Hedi Slimane in 2007 and brought an unexpected steadiness to the house, which otherwise saw a churn of womenswear and couture creative directors. He took Slimane's Dior Homme with its spindly, too-skinny tailoring and gnarly indie rock edge and evolved its output, refining it and aligning it more obviously with luxury. He allowed Slimane's out-all-night rock brat to grow up, read a book, and develop into a more vulnerable, romantic and intelligent man.

Van Assche was a small-town boy, growing up in Londerzeel, Belgium, in the flat, lonely farmlands north of Brussels, and studied womenswear at the Royal Academy of Fine Arts Antwerp. There is a reason why Van Assche was so in tune with Slimane's popular Dior Homme vibe: he interned at Yves Saint Laurent before he became an assistant to Slimane for ready-to-wear Rive Gauche Homme. When Slimane moved to Dior, Van Assche went along too.

At the helm of Dior Homme, Van Assche played with street-style influences, sportswear and logo-heavy must-haves, and his own version of the 'ugly sneaker' craze, and was able to 'subvert everyday menswear with smart sensuality', as TJ Sidhu wrote in *The Face* in 2023; the designer 'wanted his men to revel in refinement'. In the interview, Van Assche told Sidhu: 'I've always liked the idea of making an effort … My grandma used to tell me that dressing up and looking good was a form of politeness. That when you feel miserable, there's no point in putting that on everybody else. You don't need to share your misery – just dress up and look good.'

*Van Assche created a Bar Jacket
for men, drawing on Christian Dior's
ground-breaking women's silhouette.*

In 2017, Van Assche did what Dior's other men's creatives could not:
he created a Bar Jacket for men, drawing on Christian Dior's ground-
breaking women's silhouette and masculinising it with a cinched blazer.
At a time when unstructured street-style silhouettes dominated, Van
Assche remained quietly confident: 'All of the cool kids that come in
their loose streetwear clothing try on our suiting and they love it,'
he said in 2018. 'We push back against this idea that tailoring is over …'

In the end, Van Assche's quiet, small 'c' conservatism and subtle
humour won out. He departed the house in 2018 for Berluti, which
produces upmarket menswear, shoes and accessories, and published
a retrospective book of his work in 2023. 'My aim,' he said, 'and it's not
for me to judge whether I've succeeded, has always been to be right
in the middle trying to make wearable clothes that have a good dose
of creativity.'

AND JUST LIKE THAT

SJP in vintage Dior

Although there are many of us who could earn a PhD in the minutiae of the cult TV show *Sex and the City* (*SATC*), together with its sequel, *And Just Like That*, it should be up to megafans Chelsea Fairless and Lauren Garroni, creators of the podcast and viral Instagram account *Every Outfit on SATC*, to give us their take on the iconic look. In *SATC* season 3, episode 17 ('What Goes Around Comes Around'), messy main character Carrie Bradshaw (played by Sarah Jessica Parker) wears a bias-cut dress in a rare Christian Dior Daily print, introduced by Galliano in the 2000–01 autumn/winter collection.

'We can all agree that this John Galliano for Christian Dior newsprint dress is the f***ing LOOK,' write the *Every Outfit* duo. 'However, surprising an acquaintance whose marriage you destroyed in this dress is NOT. The Dior newsprint dress has a sordid history ... Galliano lifted the idea from a brilliant 1935 Elsa Schiaparelli print comprised of her own press clippings.'

'JOHN GALLIANO
THINKS ABOUT FASHION
SHOWS THE WAY
STEVEN SPIELBERG
THINKS ABOUT MOVIES;
HE BELIEVES IN SPECTACLE,
COMPLICATION, SUSPENSE.'

Michael Specter

THE SUCCESSORS

Raf Simons

In 1989, while studying industrial and furniture design at the LUCA School of Arts in Belgium, the black-clad Raf Simons interned for fashion rave bear and cult designer Walter Van Beirendonck. 'I always thought that fashion was a bit superficial, all glitz and glamour,' Simons told *The Gentlewoman* magazine in 2016, but Van Beirendonck took him to his first fashion show, Martin Margiela's 1990 all-white spring collection, and it blew Simons' mind. 'This show changed everything for me. I walked out of it and I thought, that's what I'm going to do. That show is the reason I became a fashion designer.'

He made good on that promise in 1991, when he created a graduate collection of furniture influenced by fashion – bejewelled cupboards with corsetry-style detailing – to draw the eye of Linda Loppa, the head of fashion at the Royal Academy of Fine Arts Antwerp. Only she didn't give him what he wanted, a place at the academy, but instead encouraged him to self-train as a menswear designer. Submerged in his own inspiring and art-edged community with fellow Antwerpians Véronique Branquinho and Olivier Rizzo, Simons launched his own menswear collection in 1995, exploring youth culture via his trademark creative moodiness.

What became clear over the next decade was that Simons could do just about anything. While his eponymous brand became the last word in cool, he edited magazines and books, taught fashion students, curated exhibitions, collaborated with artists, and his Belgian waffle recipe, once published by *i-D* magazine, is a masterpiece. Simons joined the German house of Jil Sander to design both menswear and womenswear in 2005, bringing sexy back to the at-times, austere brand.

Simons 'reworked the timeless codes of Dior with his refined, minimalist signature'.

When Dior began looking for a couture successor to John Galliano in 2011, assistant designer Bill Gaytten created four collections for the house, but eventually, in 2012, Raf Simons took on the top spot. The house notes that Simons 'reworked the timeless codes of Dior with his refined, minimalist signature'. His debut show was decked out with an avalanche of flowers by his favourite florist, Mark Colle, reinterpreting 'Christian Dior's flower-woman with her gracious curves, transforming her into an architectural silhouette'.

The collection was a success, and it became clear that Simons's approach might be more romantic than expected. 'I want to bring some emotion back to what I felt in the nineties,' said Raf Simons in Marc Holgate's profile for *Vogue* in 2012, just after his debut, 'because I see a lot of amazing clothes, but I don't see a lot of emotion now.' Holgate emphasised just how much was riding on Simons to ensure the house's success: 'Dior, an esteemed component of the French cultural establishment, and therefore of national pride, is relying on the belief that Simons will be the designer to rejuvenate its sense of beauty, and – a factor not to be underestimated – declare its standing in the world.'

Frédéric Tcheng's 2014 feature documentary *Dior and I* is another Raf Simons touchstone, which involved Tcheng following the designer for eight weeks before his debut couture show. There are highs, lows, drama and tears, and the film is beloved for its honest, human depiction of a creative and couture's most talented artisans as they race to the finish line. Simons moved on in 2015, and his lasting legacy – as seen on screen in *Dior and I* – is that he reinstated Christian Dior's original codes, the living spirit of the house itself.

GIRL'S TRIP

Jennifer Lawrence

An Oscar-winning actress, and an accidental pratfall, helped a gown from Raf Simons' 2013 haute couture spring collection become an overnight icon. One of the show's finale dresses – a voluminous, pink bell-shaped gown inspired by flowers – was worn by actress Jennifer Lawrence at the 85th Academy Awards. On her way up to accept best actress for her role in *Silver Linings Playbook,* she famously tripped, the dress deflating like a soufflé. Proving that there is nothing more endearing than being a good sport, Lawrence laughed sheepishly, and the dress became fashion history.

'I DON'T WANT TO SHOW CLOTHES, I WANT TO SHOW MY ATTITUDE, MY PAST, PRESENT AND FUTURE. I USE MEMORIES AND FUTURE VISIONS AND TRY TO PLACE THEM IN TODAY'S WORLD.'

Raf Simons

THE SUCCESSORS

Maria Grazia Chiuri

'When the lights went down for Chiuri's first-ever Dior catwalk back in September 2016,' remembered the *Guardian*'s Jess Cartner-Morley in 2023, 'the audience expected a new look … What we got, instead, was a new set of values.' Maria Grazia Chiuri offered fashion allied with feminism.

In 2016, seven decades after its founding, the House of Dior finally appointed its first female creative director, the designer's designer, Maria Grazia Chiuri. Naturally, Chiuri has alluded to the house's tenuous relationship with feminism in her work. The designer's book *Her Dior* (2021) celebrates more than 30 female photographers who have documented the work of the house, and her famous slogan T-shirts quoting well-known feminist minds are delightfully disruptive, but Chiuri's reach goes much further. In 2022 the *Washington Post* commended her for 'bringing Dior out of the patriarchy', and Rachel Tashjian in *Harper's Bazaar* noted her celebration of artists and thinkers around the world. Chiuri's appetite for collaboration included Kyiv-based artist Olesia Trofymenko, to whom she reached out shortly after Russia's invasion of Ukraine to commission her to make an artwork for Dior's 2022 autumn couture show. 'It was a little bit unreal,' Trofymenko said, 'because it was the first month of war and a really hard time … So it was like a message from another reality.'

If Chiuri's outlook – an easy intellectualism celebrating female creativity – brings fashion closer to youthful social justice issues, it has also kept the financiers happy. According to Cartner-Morley, revenues have tripled to €6.6 million.

*'Everybody was so surprised
when I became the first woman
in charge,' she told Cartner-Morley.*

Before joining Dior, Chiuri had spent most of her working life
(over 17 years) at Valentino, eight of those in the brand's creative top
spot alongside Pierpaolo Piccioli, her beloved collaborator. As a child,
she had grown up close to fashion because her mother had a small
womenswear boutique in Rome, and she went on to graduate from
Istituto Europeo di Design before joining Fendi. In fact, Chiuri was
the designer who created Fendi's iconic Baguette bag in the 1990s –
no small feat. Yet when Chiuri joined Dior, to some she seemed almost
unknown. At a time when fashion designers foster their own celebrity
personas, 'Everybody was so surprised when I became the first woman
in charge,' she told Cartner-Morley. 'Nobody spoke about the fact that
I had been working in fashion since I was 20.'

Along with emphasising the House of Dior's links with artists
and creatives, Chiuri has brought a sense of fun to the brand, bringing
back big hitters like the Saddle Bag, raising sales, and celebrating
the women who wear her clothes. In July 2019 she was awarded the
Légion d'honneur, just like her eminent predecessor, Christian Dior.

'YOU MUST ALWAYS BE COURAGEOUS. DON'T LET OTHERS DEFINE WHO YOU ARE.'

Maria Grazia Chiuri

T-SHIRT INSPIRATION

'We should all be feminists'

The celebrated debut Dior collection of Maria Grazia Chiuri in September 2016 is remembered not for its romantic dresses, but for a single, headline-grabbing item. A simple white slogan T-shirt with the Chimamanda Ngozi Adichie quote 'We should all be feminists' was the 'one piece that will have the fashion world talking', predicted Stef Yotka in *Vogue*, and she was right. 'Paired with an embellished midnight blue tulle skirt and sneakers, [the T-shirt] instantly became the most Instagrammed moment of the entire show.'

Later, Dior announced that a percentage of proceeds from the sale of each shirt would go to the Clara Lionel Foundation, a non-profit organisation founded by Dior ambassador Rihanna, which invests in education, disaster preparedness and medicine. Instantly popular and, as the house must have foreseen, extremely easy to copy, the shirt went into production anyway, Chiuri clearly believing the message was powerful enough to pass on.

THE
NEW
AGE

CHAPTER SEVEN

(2017–Present)

RED-CARPET
BAD GAL

Rihanna in Cannes

In May 2017, the House of Dior concocted an unforgettable fashion moment. Rihanna, already an ambassador for the brand, was due to visit the Cannes Film Festival for the very first time. The event is all about spritzes in the sun, overpriced hotel rooms, lost lanyards and the red carpet. Given Rihanna's fame, the Dior creative teams knew they had to create something otherworldly, so set about designing her a white, strapless, trumpet-shaped bustier gown, adding a matching coat with louche rolled-up sleeves and a train that draped along the ground.

The essence of this dreamy, voluptuous look was its demureness, and many noted it was something of a surprise to see Rihanna – at that point in her career – in something so classic. The outfit had a confident simplicity that seemed almost refreshing, even with its bridal vibes. It was styled with Chopard's massive emerald rings and diamond bracelets snaking up her wrists, and the whole look found itself subverted with Ri's bright red nails and a pair of delightfully ugly white *Matrix*-style sunnies by Andy Wolf Eyewear. The movie screening – Boon Joon Ho's *Okja* – might have faded from the mind somewhat, but Rihanna walking the red carpet in Dior couture is legendary.

DIOR MEN

Kim Jones

When Kim Jones graduated from London's Central Saint Martins school of art in 2002, his graduate collection was snapped up by John Galliano. He started his own menswear line in 2003, but it was his consultancy work for big commercial brands, such as sportswear giant Umbro, that earned Jones his solid, market-aware reputation. He could 'spot the razor-thin line between what a label needed to stay fresh and what it needed to stay solvent', wrote Thom Bettridge in *GQ* in 2019, and Jones soon won a role at traditional Brit brand Dunhill. He told Bettridge he was the only one of 40 candidates to reference the Dunhill archive. This seems to be key to Jones' incredible design success: a blending of the traditional and super-fresh that amounts to a highly desirable creative fence-sitting. 'He is part of a new generation of designers,' wrote Thomas Chatterton Williams in the *New York Times Style Magazine*, 'one distinguished as much by their talent as by their willingness to adapt to shifting business imperatives.'

After three years at Dunhill, Jones was picked by Marc Jacobs to lead menswear at Louis Vuitton, and for eight years Jones churned it out, relying on social media such as Instagram, and visiting Louis Vuitton stores around the world, to measure each collection's market response. By the time he moved to the House of Dior in 2018, his streetwear-influenced take on luxury was established. On Jones's watch, menswear has boomed.

His Dior Men collections make full use of the designer's capricious take on culture, buying in popular artists to create a show centrepiece or collaborate on limited-edition pieces. He's also a collecting geek, fiendishly amassing rare magazines, books, sneakers, 1970s club clothes, and Leigh Bowery accessories.

Jones' winning approach is finding the perfect balance between old and new, big name art stars, limited-edition projects and charting the buzz on social media.

Jones has long been a fan of streetwear must-have Supreme, having worked at one of the brand's distributors – the celebrated London outfit Gimme Five – in his first fashion role. Supreme are masters at creating hype through limited-edition releases and artful collaborations that translate into long queues outside Supreme boutiques around the world, online waiting lists, and a feverish fan base. Kim Jones' trick has been to borrow some of Supreme's business magic, applying it to the luxury fashion house, and having fun with fashion and art icons, such as Shawn Stussy, Kaws and Nike. 'Dior is all about the clothes; at the heart of it is silhouette, shape, technique and fabrication of the very highest order,' said Jones of his 2024 spring/summer collection, as quoted in *i-D* magazine. 'I like to think that in my five years of being here, I have not forgotten this.' But despite what he claims, Jones's approach is so much more than just clothes and accessories. His wider, winning approach – finding the perfect balance between old and new, big name art stars, limited-edition projects, charting the buzz on social media – has made big business out of Dior Men.

In 2020 Jones took the surprising step of becoming artistic director of Maria Grazia Chiuri's old haunt, Fendi, overseeing haute couture, ready-to-wear and fur collections for women (the latter still going strong, for some reason), while remaining in the Dior Men top spot.

THROWING A LOOK

Elle Fanning at Cannes

The Cannes Film Festival is less about the art of cinema and more about throwing a look (with some seriously archaic dress codes: stilettos were a must-wear for women until recent times). Some celebrities have that firmly in mind as they arrive on the red carpet in the south of France sunshine, attempting to raise their profiles – and that of their movies, of course.

In 2019 Elle Fanning wore an eye-popping 1950s-inspired look to a screening of *Once Upon a Time in Hollywood*. Her Dior haute couture ensemble consisted of a white organza shirt, dark blue tulle skirt, and a black macramé wide-brim hat, all which Dior said took 450 hours to create. The skirt, an astonishing 50 metres of tulle, took 200 hours, while the shirt, with its David Bowie in *Labyrinth*-sense of theatricality, took 150 hours.

A GLIMPSE
BACK IN TIME

Mrs Harris Goes to Paris

The charming romantic comedy *Mrs Harris Goes to Paris* (2022) – based on Paul Gallico's 1958 novel *Mrs 'Arris Goes to Paris* – involved the director Anthony Fabian, costume designer Jenny Beavan, production designer Luciana Arrighi and set decorator Nora Talmaier in recreating an early Christian Dior show at 30 Avenue Montaigne with stunning historical accuracy, right down to the blooms in the Dior salons. Lesley Manville is the lowly London house cleaner who 'falls madly, inexplicably in love with a Dior dress', wrote Rachel Tashjian in *Harper's Bazaar*. The titular Mrs Harris saves up every penny she can and heads to the House of Dior in Paris to purchase her desired couture creation, named Temptation, but her low social status sees her struggle to realise her dream in this fish-out-of-water story.

The 'film encapsulates the irrational, magical pull that fashion has on the imagination,' said Tashjian, 'and the way we might behave ridiculously in pursuit of a great dress.' It was a coup to work with production designer Luciana Arrighi, 'who in fact modeled for Yves Saint Laurent and visited the Dior atelier'. What's more, Beavan trained with the Dior artisans to create a couture gown from scratch. The movie is an unexpected delight.

THE NEW
AMBASSADORS

Kim Ji-Soo

In 2022 Maria Grazia Chiuri extended her support of female talent to Kim Ji-Soo (known as Jisoo), who was appointed an official ambassador for Dior, having become off-the-scale famous through her all-female pop outfit Blackpink. The announcement delighted Jisoo's fans (she has 76.2 million followers on Instagram alone) and shed some light on Chiuri's themes for Dior's 2021 autumn/winter collection in the Galerie des Glaces at the Palace of Versailles (Jisoo was one of the designer's inspirations). It made sense that Chiuri and Jisoo made it official: a Dior Instagram post in the months before the announcement featuring the Blackpink singer had an outsized Media Impact Value (MIV is an algorithmic dark art that seeks to measure the impact of a social media post in cold, hard cash). Bringing on Jisoo – and her legion of fans – was a no-brainer.

FASHION AFTER
THE PANDEMIC
Anya Taylor-Joy at the Golden Globes

The Golden Globes in 2021 were a tentative step back into the world
of glamour that had been so lacking during the Covid lockdowns
of the year before. Anya Taylor-Joy won the best actress award for
her role as Beth Harmon in *The Queen's Gambit* (which also won
best limited series).

'For the bombshell look,' wrote *Vogue*'s Liana Satenstein,
'Taylor-Joy worked with image architect Law Roach and Dior creative
director Maria Grazia Chiuri to realize the striking green Lurex gown
and accompanying cape … dripping with glamour.' The outfit had
a retro, 1970s disco siren feel, with fine straps and a draped bust,
accessorised with what they call in the business a 'truckload of ice'.
The Tiffany jewels were valued at more than $1 million: a platinum
and diamond pendant ($195,000), platinum and diamond earrings
($1,500,000), and a platinum and diamond ring ($130,000).

GATEWAY TO INDIA
Dior and Mumbai

'There was something quite mind-blowing about the whole experience,' said *Vogue*'s Sarah Mower, 'of being present at Maria Grazia Chiuri's introduction to India – or rather, to her making visible all of the many ways that Christian Dior is interlinked with the artisanship centred in Mumbai.' For Dior's huge 2023 pre-fall collection (some 99 looks), Chiuri invited the fashion press and their influencer counterparts to the historic Gateway of India in Mumbai, in part to show off the house's deep connection with the city, but also to remind us all where our clothes truly come from, who made them, and how.

On the trip, Mower was able to meet Chanakya Ateliers' Karishma Swali, with whom Chiuri has worked for almost 30 years. As she took over the top spot at the House of Dior, Chiuri commissioned textile murals from female artists to adorn the walls of Dior couture shows in Paris, and Swali created the Chanakya Foundation school 'which educates women in crafts and opportunities in a largely male-dominated field'.

THE HOMECOMING

Prince Harry at the Coronation

In 2023, Prince Harry, Duke of Sussex, returned to England from his California home for the coronation of King Charles III. Harry's relationship with the British press, and apparently with his family too, had never been more strained. All eyes were on the prince, desperate to read meaning into every detail of his stance, seating placement and outfit. For the historic event, Harry chose British designer Kim Jones of Dior Men to custom design a traditional three-piece suit. Given his mother's and wife's relationship with the house, it seemed fitting for the prince to fly the flag of Dior for the big day. 'In the ateliers,' said Dior via social media, 'the wool and mohair tailcoat, vest [waistcoat] and trousers custom designed by Kim Jones were constructed with traditional hand tailoring techniques.' Not everyone loved Harry's French couture look. One Twitter user wrote that there was 'bad tailoring up the inseam and he was a rumpled mess'.

EPHEMERAL ARCHITECTURE:

Dior's enduring gift to the world

If he hadn't made dresses, Christian Dior would have built buildings. Architecture was the designer's noble *faiblesse* (weakness) and, 'prevented from ever gratifying this passion, I found an outlet for it in couture', he wrote in his quippy autobiography *Dior by Dior* (1956). In the years before his death, he set about renovating an old mill house on his Milly-la-Forêt estate, and his first act was to chop off its embellishments with an axe. He then whitewashed the walls so the interiors were a clean, blank page. This was always Dior's starting point, the empty sketchbook waiting to be filled with his stunning, otherworldly imaginings. With no little effort, Dior's post-war New Look spirited itself onto the paper, followed by ground-breaking couture shapes, a princess's birthday frock, ideas for a fragrance inspired by his heroic sister, and so much more. These key creations embody the House of Dior's hallmarks – the mysterious embroidered language in which the iconic fashion house communicates.

Christian Dior's sketches, toiles and fully realised creations – even his unembellished mill house – have become an endless source of inspiration for his successors, from Yves Saint Laurent's avant-garde designs to Marc Bohan's three decades of quietly confident successes, to Gianfranco Ferré's architectural splendour. Then came John Galliano's high camp and high drama that embodied the excesses of the 1990s and 2000s, before Raf Simons's artful restraint, and then Maria Grazia Chiuri's clever refocus on the House of Dior's true inspiration: the women who wear its clothes. Perhaps Dior was something of a builder after all: 'I think of my work as ephemeral architecture,' he wrote, 'dedicated to the beauty of the female body.'

ABOUT THE AUTHOR & ILLUSTRATOR/ ACKNOWLEDGEMENTS

Dan Jones

Dan Jones is a British writer and editor living in New York. Formerly of *i-D* magazine and *Time Out London*, he's an expert in style, cocktails and queer mythology. He is the author of a number of books including one of the previous titles in this series, *Style Icon: Diana*.

Sandra Suy

Currently based in Barcelona, Sandra Suy has been working as a freelance illustrator for more than 10 years with an emphasis on fashion and beauty. She believes in the strength of details and simplicity as a means to achieve maximum expressiveness. She enjoys experimenting with textures, superimpositions, prints and collage, but always tries to maintain minimalism in the image. Less is more.

Sandra finds inspiration in all kinds of creative expressions including music, fashion, art, books and nature.

Thanks to

Chelsea Edwards, Max Edwards, Tom McDonald, Sandra Suy, Claire Warner, Trish Burgess and Clare Double.

INDEX

Published in 2024 by Hardie Grant Books,
an imprint of Hardie Grant Publishing

Hardie Grant Books (London)
5th & 6th Floors
52–54 Southwark Street
London SE1 1UN

Hardie Grant Books (Melbourne)
Building 1, 658 Church Street
Richmond, Victoria 3121

hardiegrantbooks.com

Etchings on the following pages are by Nicolas Robert
(1614–85), courtesy of the Wellcome Collection:
Page 18: *An anemone and lily: flowering stems with butterfly*
(detail); page 50: *A Christmas rose or black hellebore:
flowering stem* (detail); page 68: *A Turk's cap, a harebell and
a pansy: flowering stems* (detail); page 84: *A lily: flowering
stem with a butterfly* (detail); page 102: *A violet: flowering
stem* (detail); page 134: *A lily: flowering stem with butterfly,
moth and beetle* (detail); page 142: *Three daffodils, including
the wild daffodil: flowering stems with a butterfly* (detail).

British Library Cataloguing-in-Publication Data.
A catalogue record for this book
is available from the British Library.

Dior: Style Icon

ISBN: 978-1-78488-740-7

Publishing Director: Kajal Mistry
Senior Project Editor: Chelsea Edwards
Design: Claire Warner Studio
Copy Editor: Trish Burgess
Proofreader: Clare Double
Indexer: Helen Snaith
Production Controller: Martina Georgieva

Colour Reproduction by p2d
Printed and bound in China by Leo Paper Products Ltd
10 9 8 7 6 5 4 3 2 1

MIX
Paper | Supporting
responsible forestry
FSC™ C020056